The Lost Art of Generosity

How Honor
Leads To Prosperity

Daniel T. Newton

Resources by Daniel Newton and Grace Place Ministries:

Truth in Tension: 55 Days to Living in Balance

Immeasurable: Reviewing the Goodness of God

Never Give Up: The Supernatural Power of Christlike Endurance

The Lost Art of Discipleship

The Lost Art of Discipleship Workbook

The Lost Art of Perseverance

All Things

It Is Finished

The Lost Art of Faith Righteousness

The Lost Art of Fasting

The Lost Art of Selfless Love

The Lost Art of Rest

The Lost Art of Excellence

The Lost Art of Friendship

The Lost Art of Confrontation

The Lost Art of Deliverance Ministry

The Lost Art of Meditation

The Lost Art of Praying in Tongues

The Lost Art of Generosity

GP Music: Beginnings – Worship Album

For more information on these books
and other inspiring resources, visit us at
www.GracePlaceMedia.com

Table of Contents

Introduction

When you think of heaven, you may picture the sea of glass, streets of gold, buildings adorned in precious stones, angels in flowing robes, and God sitting on His throne arrayed in glory and majesty. Heaven is a place without striving, toiling, poverty, or lack. Yet, why is it that when many think about Christians, the very ambassadors of His kingdom, they think of people who are always looking for a handout?

Many churches seem to be constantly raising money, yet never have enough for their needs. Instead of abundance, there is stinginess, self-protection, and fear of lack throughout the Body of Christ. Jesus told us to pray, "Your kingdom come. Your will be done on earth as it is in heaven" (Matt. 6:10), but why do we see the exact opposite of that reality?

"For I know the plans I have for you,' declares the Lord, 'plans to prosper you and not to harm you, plans to give you hope and a future.'"
- Jeremiah 29:11 NIV

It doesn't matter what part of the world I go to. When I mention "prosperity," I either excite or offend people. Years of poor biblical teaching, pressure to give, and exploitation have led many to be turned off by this truth. It's become a dirty word to many believers. However, it's clear throughout Scripture that God wants us to prosper and abound in every area of our lives. His will for us is that we would see heaven manifest here and now. If there is no lack in His kingdom, there shouldn't be any in our lives either.

God is not toiling and striving, hoping that He will have enough for us. His desire is for us to abound in all things, and He can certainly make that happen. Yet how does He choose to do it? The Lord leads us into prosperity through generosity, and true biblical generosity is an act of honor. These three themes—honor, generosity, and prosperity—are deeply interconnected. Honor leads to generosity, and generosity leads to prosperity.

When we recognize how much we've been freely given, generosity will come naturally to us. Jesus says it's more blessed to give than receive (see Acts 20:35). Our God is generous, and to represent Him rightly, we must also be generous. It's crucial that we recognize the power and necessity of being generous believers. Not only will it destroy lack in our lives, but it will cause us to walk in the prosperity He's prepared for us. The Lord desires to bless us, not only for us but so that we can be a blessing to those around us!

Generosity has become a lost art, but it doesn't have to stay that way. It's time we give generously and watch as He abundantly provides for us. It's time we rediscover The Lost Art of Generosity.

Part 1

Biblical Generosity

Chapter 1

"Heaven's Economy"

"For My thoughts are not your thoughts, Nor are your ways My ways,' says the LORD. 'For as the heavens are higher than the earth, So are My ways higher than your ways, And My thoughts than your thoughts.'"
- Isaiah 55:8-9

Jesus was not your conventional rabbi. Whether He was spitting in dirt and rubbing it in someone's eyes or flipping tables in the temple, saying He had a different way of doing things would be an understatement. The Lord operates differently than we do, and His methods are better than ours. As this scripture says, His thoughts and ways are higher than ours, and one thing we can know for sure is that He will not adjust Himself to our standards; He calls us to align with His.

Jesus teaches us to seek His kingdom first. When we do, He promises that all of our needs will be met (see Matt. 6:33). However, worldly wisdom teaches us to take care of ourselves first. It causes us to be more loyal to money than we are to the Lord. Jesus says in Matthew 6:24, "No one can serve two masters; for either he will hate the one and love the other, or else he will be loyal to the one and despise the other. You cannot serve God and mammon."

In Bible times, the word "mammon" was used to describe money, riches, and material wealth. It is the economic system of the world. It teaches us to serve ourselves but is cursed with toil and self-reliance. It constantly leads us to search for a method or formula to achieve success, but it's entirely based on self. Whether it's about how much money we've made or how we've performed in our lives, mammon causes our focus to be placed on ourselves and our ability. So, the question is, how can we break away from trusting in worldly wisdom to walking in God's divine structure for our lives? The answer is through faith.

The Currency of Heaven

Everyone loves a good formula. *If I do A and B, then add C, it will always equal D.* We like formulas because they make us feel in control. However, we as believers are not called to trust in 10-step programs or man-made methods. Where the world's system is based on self-effort and striving, the Lord's standard is faith.

Faith is the currency of God's kingdom realm. It requires us to depend entirely on the Lord and trust in Him. We were saved through faith (see Eph. 2:8). We are called to walk by faith (see 2 Cor. 5:7). Everything God has called us to do is built on this foundation of believing and trusting.

"Command those who are rich in this present age not to be haughty, nor to trust in uncertain riches but in the living God, who gives us richly all things to enjoy."
- 1 Timothy 6:17

What does it mean to trust? Trusting in something means placing confidence in or relying on it. If I sit down in a chair, I am putting trust in its ability to hold my weight. It's the same with our attempts to accumulate wealth, whether by storing up savings, investing in stocks, or simply working overtime to make more. These actions demonstrate our value and trust in the world's economy.

However, what would happen if our currency were to lose its value? Even if you had a ton of money, what would it matter anymore? This is why this scripture says we're not called to trust (place confidence) in uncertain riches or money but in God. When we trust Jesus to be our source, we can experience the true richness of all things. When we trust in ourselves, we settle for a far lesser experience. Either way, it's up to us. We can hold on to our material possessions and money, or we can hold on to Jesus.

The Love of Money

"For the love of money is the root of all evil..."
- 1 Timothy 6:10 KJV

When we trust in the Lord, we should believe that He wants us to prosper, and part of that is having money. *Wait just a second, Daniel. Doesn't the Bible say money is the root of all evil?* Actually, no. The Bible says it is the *love of* money that is the root of all evil. We can appreciate financial blessings from the Lord while not loving the money itself. It's important to distinguish this rightly because if we're not careful, we'll end up throwing the baby out with the bathwater.

Money is neutral, neither good nor evil. However, it is a resource that the Lord uses to bless us and others through us. As we will discover throughout this book, God's plan was never just about blessing us in our spiritual lives but also in our physical lives as well. Blessing and prosperity are a part of His divine plan for every area of our lives (see Jer. 29:11). The more we believe that He is our extravagantly generous Father, the more we can trust that He will bless us. The key is remembering that He is the source of our prosperity, and we are not.

A problem I've seen is that many believers lean on worldly wisdom for their finances more than the Word of God. It's not even that principles such as saving or investing are necessarily wrong, but they are not the complete picture of God's plan. Where the world places a greater value on accumulation, the Lord values generosity.

Sowing and Reaping

"Give, and it will be given to you: good measure, pressed down, shaken together, and running over will be put into your bosom. For with the same measure that you use, it will be measured back to you."

- Luke 6:38

This scripture is profound because it reveals a divine principle of generosity. When you give, it will be given back to you in abundance! He isn't the God of "just enough." He is El Shaddai, the God of more than enough! So, when you give, no matter what it is you're giving, abundance will come back to you. Generosity attracts favor and increase because every time you give, you are actually sowing a seed.

I've often heard people say they don't give with the intention of getting back. As noble as that may sound, it's contrary to Scripture. Not only that, but have you ever heard of a farmer who planted seeds but didn't expect a harvest? Don't you think that would be a little strange? When we sow seed, it should be normal to expect a harvest. Yet, it seems like many people don't want to expect something back after they've sown seeds. It's almost as if they're afraid to admit they desire blessings or think it is less virtuous to be motivated by rewards. Yet, even Jesus persevered in His call for a reward. Hebrews 12:2 says that it was for the joy set before Him that He endured the Cross!

On the other hand, many people seem to want the harvest, but they aren't planting any seeds. If we understand the principle of sowing and reaping, we should anticipate harvest every time we sow seed. The more we do, the more eager we will be to give because we know we will reap a harvest.

As we continue on this journey, I desire to share what God has taught me through His Word. He desires to prosper us and make us abound, but it's not by worldly wisdom or methods. It's simply by being generous as He is generous. When we see ourselves as farmers and sowers of seed, we will joyfully plant more so we can reap more. However, before we can properly develop a value for generosity in our lives, we first have to understand the principle of honor as the Bible describes it to be.

Chapter 2

Honor

Many believers are familiar with the idea of honor, but do we really know what it means? To understand how the word 'honor' is used throughout the Bible, we must first understand it in its original context. After all, the writers of the New Testament were not writing in English but in Greek. The Greek word for honor is *timaó*, which means "to fix the value, to price."

"For you were bought at a price; therefore glorify God in your body and in your spirit, which are God's."
- 1 Corinthians 6:20

"For God commanded, saying, 'Honor your father and your mother'; and, 'He who curses father or mother, let him be put to death.'"
- Matthew 15:4

The word "price" Paul uses in 1 Corinthians 6:20 is the same word used in Matthew 15:4 when it says to *honor* your father and mother. What this shows us is that honor should cost something. We were purchased at a price, and that shows what our value is.

This is why what God did for us at Calvary is so significant. He paid the highest price—His Son, Jesus. God paid for us with His life, and He deserves the costly price of our lives in return.

Honor is Giving

"A son honors his father, and a slave his master. If I am a father, where is the honor due me? If I am a master, where is the respect due me?' says the Lord Almighty. 'It is you priests who show contempt for my name. But you ask, 'How have we shown contempt for your name?' 'By offering defiled food on my altar.' But you ask, 'How have we defiled you?' 'By saying that the Lord's table is contemptible. When you offer blind animals for sacrifice, is that not wrong? When you sacrifice lame or diseased animals, is that not wrong? Try offering them to your governor! Would he be pleased with you? Would he accept you?' says the Lord Almighty."

- Malachi 1:6-8 NIV

In Malachi, the Lord was angry because He was not receiving proper honor from His people. Their words made it *seem* like they honored Him, but they were offering blind, lame, and sick animals as sacrifices. God deserved a greater and more costly sacrifice that showed their respect. To Him, honor is more than just *saying* it with words—it requires action. Words find their full weight in the actions that back them up.

"Honor the LORD with your possessions, and with the firstfruits of all your increase; so your barns will be filled with plenty, and your vats will overflow with new wine."

- Proverbs 3:9-10

14

Whenever you see someone in Scripture giving an offering to the Lord, it is a direct indication of their honor toward Him. When someone honored the Lord, they showed it by giving the best of their wealth and possessions. True honor always results in giving.

When I first discovered this in the Word, I started blessing my mom financially much more. When I reflected on everything my mom had done for me, I couldn't help but want to bless her. Sure, I had told her many times how grateful I was for her over the years, but when I saw that honor meant to give, I knew I needed to do something. If the Word says to honor our parents so that our days will be well and long upon the earth, then I want to obey and follow what it says to do.

Honor Leads to Impartation

"He who gives honour to a prophet, in the name of a prophet, will be given a prophet's reward; and he who gives honour to an upright man, in the name of an upright man, will be given an upright man's reward."

- Matthew 10:41 BBE

I've learned so much from my mom and her relationship with Jesus. I honor her very much, and because of this, I have been able to receive abundantly from her life. A fundamental principle in God's kingdom is that the more we honor someone, the more we can receive from that person. To the measure that you honor is to the measure that you will receive.

This principle can be applied to an endless number of scenarios. In the above scripture, Jesus tells us that when we give honor to a prophet because they are a prophet, we will receive their reward. You may not be the best speaker or business person, but when you honor others who are skilled in those areas, you will receive the blessing on their lives. The principle remains the same regardless of who a person is or the specific scenario.

When we honor, we position ourselves to receive and obtain God's blessings on another's life. Even if we don't agree with everything someone says or does, we can still receive from them because of humility and honor. Recognizing the value they bring changes our perspective of them and causes us to honor them for who God made them to be. We should believe that God's principle regarding honor is true and have the desire to receive what they carry.

Taking this even further, it's important to understand this when it comes to serving your leaders. When you are humble, you will recognize that your leaders have something that you need to learn and receive. If you don't honor them, you won't receive anything. The more you honor them by being a blessing to them, the more you can receive, grow, and be blessed yourself. I can't tell you how many seeds I've sown into ministers' lives who are more anointed, gifted, and experienced than I am. I knew they had something I needed to receive and learn. So, I showed honor where it was due. Every time I did, I saw an increase of fruit and blessing in my life.

"King Solomon gave the queen of Sheba all she desired and asked for, besides what he had given her out of his royal bounty. Then she left and returned with her retinue to her own country."

- 1 Kings 10:13 NIV

When the queen of Sheba heard about Solomon's wisdom, she decided to go and see it for herself. When she witnessed his wealth, her first response was to honor him generously. She gave him gold, spices, and precious stones. She gave so much that the Word says, "Never again were so many spices brought in as those the queen of Sheba gave to King Solomon" (1 Kings 10:10 NIV). When she honored him in that way, it says that Solomon gave her all that she asked for, plus what he'd already given her out of his own treasury. She honored him and, in the end, received more than she had even come for.

Any time you give generously from a place of honor, you will receive greater than what you sow. If Solomon was moved by her honor and generosity to give above and beyond, how much more will God be moved when we give generously?

Chapter 3

Love is Generous

The Ultimate Giver

"For God so loved the world that He gave His only begotten Son, that whoever believes in Him should not perish but have everlasting life."

-John 3:16

The Lord is our generous Father. He isn't stingy, wanting to hoard everything for Himself. On the contrary, He is so generous that He didn't withhold even His own Son, Jesus, from us (see Rom. 8:32). Our God is elaborate and bountiful in everything He does, and it is all because of His love for us.

This scripture says it was because God so *loved* us that He *gave* us Jesus. Love gives generously. Lovers are givers. In fact, the Lord Himself is love personified (see 1 John 4:8). He is the ultimate Giver and has given us the ultimate Gift. We can even see His generosity on display in our everyday lives. From the gift of life itself, the food on our tables, or the presence of our loved ones that surround us, we are generously blessed in every way!

James 1:17 says, "Every good gift and every perfect gift is from above, and comes down from the Father of lights, with whom there is no variation or shadow of turning." According to this scripture, there is nothing good or perfect we've ever received in our lives that hasn't come from Him!

Not only this, but the Lord calls us to follow His model to become as generous as He is generous. Jesus taught us, "Freely you have received, freely give" (Matt. 10:8). When we meditate on how much God has given us, how could we not freely give back to Him and others?

Fear and Lack

Often, our greatest hindrance to giving is fear. Fear is the opposite of love and will create lack in your life. If you don't believe God loves you, you will develop a fear that He won't provide for you, and you will strive to provide for yourself. It's important to understand that what we focus on is what will be magnified.

A friend of mine says, "Your thoughts are the preview of your life's coming attractions." I love this quote because I've found it to be very true. This is why being mindful of what you focus on is so important. As Proverbs 23:7 says, "For as he thinks in his heart, so is he..." (For more on this topic, check out my book, *The Lost Art of Meditation*.) If we're not careful, entertaining the fear of lack will only attract lack to us.

Fear often masquerades as wisdom, but in reality, it's a thief. Many people have fears regarding their money and possessions, which leads them to live in constant worry and control. This may ruffle some feathers, but I'll use retirement as an example.

While I'm not necessarily saying not to plan for retirement, I've seen that it's often prepared for out of fear and control. Whether it's because people are afraid of being in lack one day or of losing control of their future, I've seen many hold a tight grip on their money and possessions in the name of retirement and saving. This tight grip hinders them from living generously because they have become fearful and protective of their possessions. Fear often reveals our lack of trust in the Lord. The key to annihilating this mistrust is to know God's love.

"There is no fear in love; but perfect love casts out fear..."
- 1 John 4:18

Once we realize how loved we are by the Lord, it will eradicate any fear regarding our future. When His love casts fear out, generosity becomes normal. The Lord gave to us generously when He sent His Son to die. Because of His death and resurrection, we now have access to blessing in every area, including finances. This blessing allows us to give without having concern for ourselves.

When we're free from fear and concern, we can give with love and joy. I have a core value of living generously and constantly sowing seeds by giving. I would never want to be seen as stingy because I want to model my life after Jesus, the Giver Himself.

Something I've often done is purposefully keep myself from focusing on numbers. Often, when people obsess over the cost of things, expenses, and what they don't have, it creates worry and bondage to fear. As we've discussed, money isn't inherently evil, but if you're not careful, it will bind you through a fear of lack. It's not about what you own but what owns you. I don't want to live bound by money or fear. Ultimately, because I trust that

God loves me, I believe He will always take care of me because He is my provider.

Where's Your Focus?

I've chosen not to focus on retirement with my money because I don't plan to retire. Instead, I plan to use my entire life to advance His kingdom, live generously toward others, and walk in prosperity. I want to leave a legacy of generosity everywhere I go. Instead of being selfish with how I'm spending my money, holding onto it for myself, I would much rather give it away, sow seeds, and invest in a future reward!

When we sow seeds, they are meant to produce a harvest. Generosity produces prosperity. I'm not saying that we should be demanding or entitled. Instead, I'm simply saying we should believe God's Word and follow His principles. Once again, a farmer would be foolish to plant a seed but not have any expectation for crops to grow. Therefore, when we sow, we should do so to be a blessing, and also sow with the confidence that we will reap a harvest.

Each seed is an investment into our future. While worldly wisdom would advise us to save, save, save, God desires that we generously give, give, give, and allow Him to give back to us! Blessing others by investing our time, money, and resources can be costly, but when we understand that we are investing in them, it always pays off to produce a mighty harvest!

Biblical generosity is the pathway to prosperity. When we learn to walk in selfless love, we will give freely. When we learn to honor the Lord and others through our giving, we can be sure that there will be rewards that await us. While the world's system may have taught us otherwise, God's economy is built on faith and trust. As you continue on the journey of embracing *The Lost Art of Generosity,* you will learn to trust the Lord in every area of your life, believing that He loves you and will provide for you!

Part 2

Honoring the Lord

Chapter 4

Putting Him First

What would happen if we honored the Lord first and foremost in our lives? God deserves our first and our best, not our leftovers. As I shared earlier, we position ourselves to receive when we show honor. He's the one who owns the cattle on a thousand hills. Therefore, what blessings might we experience from Him if we brought Him the honor He deserves?

Many people think that life is about what you own. Don't get me wrong, I like having nice things. However, my number one priority is to live a life wholly pleasing to the Lord. I didn't grow up in a rich family, but I have continuously seen the blessing of God in my life. I know this is because I decided to put Him first. I can't boast about anything because I know everything I have is a gift from Him and a result of His blessing on my life.

"Therefore do not worry, saying, 'What shall we eat?' or 'What shall we drink?' or 'What shall we wear?' For after all these things the Gentiles seek. For your heavenly Father knows that you need all these things. But seek first the kingdom of God and His righteousness, and all these things shall be added to you."

- Matthew 6:31-33

When we make Him the priority in our lives, we don't have to worry about whether or not we'll have the right clothes to wear or the best food to eat. He knows what we need, and we can trust that He will provide. As we honor Him first, He promises to generously supply everything we need.

Generosity is the outflow of our trust in God. It's possible to be generous without faith, but it is impossible to have faith in God for our finances and not be generous. Faith without works is dead (see James 2:17), so faith must look like something. When we trust in Him, we can give freely because we know He will take care of us.

As we covered in Part 1, it was for the joy set before Jesus that He endured the Cross. Jesus was joyful because He knew that giving up His life would result in relationship with us. He didn't give in response to pressure; He gave cheerfully with joy!

Hilarious Giving

"So let each one give as he purposes in his heart, not grudgingly or of necessity; for God loves a cheerful giver."
- 2 Corinthians 9:7

It's a joyful experience to give because when you give, you're not relying on yourself but on God and His provision. A synonym for the word cheerful is hilarious. God loves a hilarious giver. There have been times I've laughed so hard when I gave because I didn't know where the provision for my needs would come from. Sacrificial giving seemed so ridiculous to my natural mind. Despite that, I chose to give because I knew God would bring the increase into my life as He always has! He is my source and my provider.

When I started Grace Place many years ago, my financial situation was pretty difficult. I was living paycheck to paycheck, and those were definitely not my best days. However, even when I didn't have money, I knew it was still important to give.

At the time, I had only one discipleship house with nine guys. One week, I was preparing for Family Night, our weekly gathering where we'd have dinner, share the highs and lows of our week, worship, and either a guest speaker or I would minister. Usually, we would all chip in to pay for the meal, but that night, I wanted to bless everyone by covering it all. The only problem was that I only had about forty dollars in my bank account and wasn't going to get paid for another two weeks.

Despite this, I still wanted to bless everyone, so I went to the grocery store and picked up enough salad, fried chicken, potato salad, dinner rolls, and dessert for us all to eat. The total came to be $41.65. I found another two dollars in my wallet, paid for the food, and walked out with about 35 cents left to my name.

That night, the guys were grateful for the meal, but none of them had any idea about the sacrifice it was for me. I was glad I got to bless them, but I had no clue where I was going to get money for the next two weeks. When the night was over, I parked my car outside of my house and exploded with laughter. "Lord, this is hilarious! You're going to have to provide for me because I trust you, and I did this in faith."

I walked over to my mailbox before heading inside and found a letter from my former employer. It had been two years since I worked for them, so I was caught off guard. When I opened the envelope, it read, "Dear Mr. Newton, after an audit of our accounts, we realized that we underpaid you. Enclosed is a check for $768." Only a few hours after taking a risk to be generous, the Lord surprised me with a blessing! Some may disagree, but I'm convinced that if I had partnered with fear and not been generous, that check wouldn't have been in my mailbox. I stepped out in faith, hilariously gave, and I was blessed!

The Power to Make Wealth

"And you shall remember the Lord your God, for it is He who gives you power to get wealth, that He may establish His covenant which He swore to your fathers, as it is this day."

- Deuteronomy 8:18

It is God who has given us the ability to create wealth, not ourselves. Apart from Him, we can do nothing (see John 15:5). With Him, however, we can live in the abundance He has prepared for us.

It's sad to see believers strive so hard to provide for themselves in their own strength. It's almost as if some are embarrassed to admit they're unable to live without His help. Not only is that prideful, but it's also much more work. When we completely abandon ourselves to Him, we're liberated to give joyfully! The reason many Christians aren't cheerful givers is because they think it all depends on them. They don't know the joy of trusting the Lord and honoring Him first with their finances.

When we remember the Lord, we will keep Him at the forefront of our minds, honoring Him above all else. As we do, giving will come naturally! He is worthy, and anyone who beholds Him long enough won't be able to resist giving to Him. For the Church to walk in God's fullness for us, we must give generously.

When we honor the Lord with our finances, blessing, increase, and acceleration will surely come!

Chapter 5

Types of Giving

Tithing

"Bring the whole tithe into the storehouse, so that there may be food in My house, and test Me now in this,' says the LORD of hosts, 'if I will not open for you the windows of heaven and pour out for you a blessing until it overflows. Then I will rebuke the devourer for you, so that it will not destroy the fruits of the ground; nor will your vine in the field cast its grapes,' says the LORD of hosts."

- Malachi 3:10-11 NASB 1995

Tithing is the most foundational type of biblical giving. It means "a tenth" and signifies giving a tenth of all we have to the Lord. I have always found this passage fascinating because it is the only place in Scripture that urges us to test the Lord. It is a remarkable demonstration of His generosity because, despite the fact that God has provided everything for us, He only asks that a tenth be brought back into His house. His extravagant generosity is given to us in exchange for such a small request. In Malachi, when His people withheld their tithes, the Lord was angry with them and accused them of robbery. The tithe belongs to the Lord, and it is the most basic level of giving to show honor to Him for all He's provided.

Tithing carries a great promise. The Lord invites us to test Him by tithing, saying that when we do, He will open up the windows of heaven and pour blessings out on us that we won't even be able to contain! I love this! It's almost like He is provoking us, saying, "You don't think I'm going to bless your socks off? Go ahead and try me. See what happens, I dare you!" When we tithe, we test the Lord and give Him the opportunity to prove His Word's integrity. In doing so, we secure ourselves in His provision and blessing. What matters the most is trusting Him.

Initially, tithing may seem like a minuscule discipline that doesn't require much. What many people don't anticipate is that the more income you make, the more the tithe becomes. Years ago, I taught my team about this and drew a graph to illustrate.

For example, if you currently make $20,000 a year, your annual tithe would be $2,000. Divided over 12 months, that would be around $166 each month. This doesn't seem like that much, right? However, later in life, let's say you work hard to advance your career and make $150,000 a year. That's awesome! However, what you may not have expected was that your annual tithe just became $15,000, which is $1,250 each month. Do you see what happened? It may not have seemed that much at first, but as your income increases, the tithe also continues to grow. Suddenly, you may say, "Wow. This is a lot more than I was thinking!"

However, as our tithe increases, so should our trust in the Lord. It's important to develop that perspective so we can become cheerful givers. The more we think like this, the more excited we'll be to step beyond the bare minimum and give even more!

Sacrificial Giving

Some people debate about whether tithing is even required today. I would say yes, it is. However, not only is tithing essential, but from what I've seen in Scripture, generosity is far more crucial. I once heard Pastor Bill Johnson say, "So, you tithe? Congratulations, you're not robbing God." I love that statement because it helps us to see that we're not called to live a bare minimum lifestyle. We're called to go above and beyond in everything we do! Where tithing is the basic, we also have the opportunity to give even more sacrificially.

"Then the king said to Araunah, 'No, but I will surely buy it from you for a price; nor will I offer burnt offerings to the Lord my God with that which costs me nothing.' So David bought the threshing floor and the oxen for fifty shekels

of silver."
- 2 Samuel 24:24

David set out to build an altar to the Lord and make a sacrifice. When he found the perfect location to build the altar, he was determined to purchase it. The person he needed to purchase it from, Araunah, offered to give him the threshing floor to build the altar on, as well as the oxen and wood for the offering. To Araunah's offer, David had a profound response. He said he would not offer something unto the Lord that cost him nothing. David understood it was not just a formality to give. Sacrificial giving comes from the heart.

God declared David to be a man after His own heart. That was because David was completely devoted to Him, to the point of giving sacrificially and generously toward Him. How much more should we, who have been saved and set free by the blood of the Lamb, also have a desire to honor the Lord in our giving?

"Now Jesus sat opposite the treasury and saw how the people put money into the treasury. And many who were rich put in much. Then one poor widow came and threw in two mites, which make a quadrans. So He called His disciples to Himself and said to them, 'Assuredly, I say to you that this poor widow has put in more than all those who have given to the treasury; for they all put in out of their abundance, but she out of her poverty put in all that she had, her whole livelihood.'"

- Mark 12:41-44

Can you imagine being in the temple when this happened? This would be highly offensive today. Some may even say that God doesn't look at *what* you give, but only cares *that* you give. Yet, here we have this story of Jesus, the Son of God, sitting and watching people put money in the offering basket. After observing what everyone gave, He even called His disciples over to tell them about it! He taught them that the widow gave more than anyone else because she took all of what she had and gave it to the Lord.

Many of the rich would put in very large sums, but a destitute widow walked up and dropped in two small copper coins worth less than a penny. This woman gave her last two mites to the Lord because she honored Him. Though she gave a fraction of what others gave, she honored the Lord with all her wealth, and it moved Him.

The amount we give doesn't matter as much as the heart behind our giving. When we honor and trust the Lord with our wealth, we will continually give even when it's difficult. When we give, we are not only giving to a person, a church, or a good work, but we are ultimately giving to the Lord.

My brother used to attend a church where their main giving message was about sacrificial giving. The church was in one of the wealthiest counties in the US, and the pastor would tell the people, "If you're a schoolteacher in this county, I don't even know if you can afford to give 10%. But most of you are not schoolteachers. You're VPs and CEOs. If you're only giving 10%, you're extremely cheap." He understood that just because you're giving large amounts doesn't mean you're giving large percentages, and it's the percentages that often reveal more of the heart.

The people's hearts were revealed with their giving. In the same way that no one would show up to a president or king empty-handed, how much more should we honor the King of Kings and Lord of Lords with our finances?

Lordship

As we've discussed, many people's issues with giving are because of their fear, control, and trust issues. However, realizing that we are not the lord of our lives makes things so much easier. There have been times that I've given out of abundance, but there were also many other times that I gave out of sacrifice. Either way, we have to get to a place where we never allow a fear of lack to hinder us from obeying the call to be generous in our giving.

God created it all, and whether we have much or a little, we must recognize that He is our source and our Lord. When we surrender our lives to Him, that also includes our finances. Lack, greed, and selfishness can only have a place when we take back the reigns over our lives. When we are surrendered to Him, the grip of control is broken, and we are set free to live in His provision. Living in the abundance that God provides is much more fulfilling than anything we could ever produce in our own ability.

Part 3

Honoring Others

Chapter 6

Selfless Giving

When our focus is honoring the Lord in all we do, generosity becomes the natural by-product. God is our provider who takes care of us, so we don't need to worry about our own needs. As we trust in His ability to provide, increase will naturally come. He's called us to be selfless, and we can only do this when we know we don't have to take care of ourselves.

Jesus poses the question that, if we know how to give good gifts, how much more does our Father in heaven (see Matt. 7:11)? He's not looking to provide us with only what we need to survive. Nothing He does is the bare minimum. He always goes above and beyond what we ask for. It's His character and nature. The more we believe this, the more we'll give every chance we get. The question is, how can we give away what we don't have?

Abundance to Bless

"I will make you a great nation; I will bless you and make your name great; And you shall be a blessing. I will bless those who bless you, and I will curse him who curses you; And in you all the families of the earth shall be blessed."

- Genesis 12:2-3

The entire reason God wanted to bless Abraham and His people was so they could have an abundance to bless the world around them. The Lord wanted to show His loving kindness to the world through the people He had blessed. He intended that they would give to the surrounding nations out of their abundance. That's how good He is.

The Lord shows His goodness through blessing, and we should want to be just like Him. Anyone who's soft-hearted and knows the Lord will desire to give. Unfortunately, some mindsets prevent us from being as generous as we've been called to be.

I've seen many Christians say they want to give but don't want to become wealthy in the process. Thinking this way makes no sense. If you want to be able to give abundantly, you have to have *abundance*. We have to stop worrying about what others think and change our mindset on what it means to be wealthy. The problem is that most of society trains us to believe that wealth is wicked.

A majority of movies portray rich people as evil, selfish, and careless to the needs of others. The rich person always seems to need the poor person to show them the real meaning of life. The good guy is often the person who works as the employee rather than the business owner. These movies paint the picture that being wealthy means you don't help others, but this couldn't be further from the truth.

I know people from all different levels of income. There are both wealthy and poor people who are kind. There are also wealthy and poor people who are stingy. We can't allow ourselves to categorize people by how much money or possessions they have.

As believers, we should want to be those who are kind and loving, and also those who are financially blessed. I don't love money, but I do love what I can do with money. I can feed the poor, travel to preach the Gospel, support others who are doing the work of the Lord, bless those I love, and so many other things. We should desire to be the wealthiest people on the planet so we can bless others.

Imagine you have extra land and find out someone needs land to build a church. You could bless them with that land, and the work of the Lord could be done. How was this possible? It was possible because you were blessed!

There may even be circumstances where the blessing opens doors of influence for you to win people's hearts. Character doesn't matter to some people because they don't have any. However, what does matter to them is money. If you are walking in the blessing of the Lord, they will notice that and respect you. As they do, you will have a voice of influence to encourage them, counsel them, and even lead them to give their lives to the Lord if they desire. When you focus your attention on blessing others, God will use you mightily because He knows He can trust you.

It is More Blessed to Give

"... remember the words of the Lord Jesus, that He said, 'It is more blessed to give than to receive.'"

- Acts 20:35

I love traveling all over the world to different countries, churches, and cultures because you can see a unique and beautiful side of God in each place. Unlike the West, I've found that some cultures never do separate checks when they go out to eat. Many years ago, while in Asia for a ministry trip, I visited an expensive restaurant with a group of people. When the bill came, I wanted to split the check because I didn't want anyone else to have to pay for my meal.

When I tried to split off my check, I could see how offensive that was to the man who wanted to pay for the entire bill. He considered it an honor and a blessing to be able to pay for everyone. He understood Jesus' words that "it is more blessed to give than to receive." He took greater enjoyment in being able to give than he did in keeping the amount of money the meal would have cost. When we understand this truth the way he did, we will walk out a life of true generosity and prosperity.

Today, many want to receive more than they want to give. Often in conversations, people ask, "What do you want in life?" "I want a nice car." "I want a big house." "I want a dog, three kids, and a loving spouse." None of these things are wrong, but why are most of our conversations about what we want? What about what we want to give?

You know someone's heart is in the right place when they say, "I want to be able to give." In order to give, you need the money to do so. However, with many people, if they had the money, they would think about what they wanted instead of blessing others.

We will never get to the place of selfless giving if we only think of our desires. We have to ask God to change our hearts in this. When we are more wowed by what we give than what we receive, we will know our hearts are in the right place. What if we started to dream more about what we could give away than what we could receive?

I remember when I was a teenager, I'd get dressed up with my friends and drive down to Baltimore to visit luxury car dealerships. We'd go in and ask to test drive the cars. I was seventeen and driving Mercedes G-Wagons and Lexuses. Dressing the part and walking in confidence got us into many nice cars.

While doing this, I remember talking with my friends about our dreams of living in giant mansions and owning sportscars. Another dream I had, however, was to someday go test-driving cars with someone who didn't know I was wealthy. After our fun, I would ask them which was their favorite and then buy that exact car for them on the spot! My dreams were focused on what I could give, not just what I could receive.

When you realize that you have to be more blessed to give, you'll desire God's blessing even more. Any abundance you have will be a joy to give away! As I said before, my family wasn't wealthy growing up, but we were very blessed. I remember how my parents would hear of people having a difficult time, and they would invite them to come stay at our house for free. This happened throughout my entire childhood. We would often have people over for dinner and host them to the best of our ability. There were even a couple of times that they blessed others by giving away their car and truck! My parents were always filled with joy as they did this, and the more we blessed others, the more we were blessed as well.

When you look to give more than you look to receive, you start a cycle of blessing in your life. Proverbs 11:25 in the NLT says, "The generous will prosper; those who refresh others will themselves be refreshed." This scripture teaches us the complete opposite of what the world teaches. We're taught that if we want to be refreshed, we should withhold ourselves. If we want to have provision, we need to save. Yet, true refreshment comes when we refresh others, and it's the generous person who will prosper and be made rich.

Dream List

I encourage you to take some time now to pause and dream with the Lord. What are you excited to give? What are some significant ways you would love to be a blessing to others? For example, maybe you would love to surprise your neighbor by buying their groceries for them. Or how about paying off someone's school tuition? There's no limit to what's possible with God! Dream big, make a list, and look for opportunities the Lord opens to make these things happen!

Where the world is teaching us one way, God is showing us His way. He never meant for the blessing to stop with us, but rather, He invites us to be just like Him, generously giving away to others. *The Lost Art of Generosity* won't be lost when we realize the pure joy that comes as we give selflessly to others, just as He has done with us.

Chapter 7

Sowing Into Others

"Now he who supplies seed to the sower and bread for food will also supply and increase your store of seed and will enlarge the harvest of your righteousness. You will be enriched in every way so that you can be generous on every occasion, and through us your generosity will result in thanksgiving to God."

- 2 Corinthians 9:10-11 NIV

As we've discussed, the blessing of the Lord was never meant to stop with us. We're blessed to be a blessing! Generosity is like a river, and as we continue to give, whether directly to the Lord or to others, we keep that current moving. That's why money is called *currency*. It's meant to flow. It's simply the way He's designed it to be.

When we have a heart postured to give generously, He will continue to provide us with the seed to sow. It's the cycle of generosity. God is generous toward us. As a result, we can be generous toward others. Then, as we are generous to bless others, the Lord will continue to bless us. The only thing that stops this is if we don't take the blessing He's given to us and give it away. If, instead, we withhold what we have, the current

49

will become stagnant.

Any time we're tempted to stop the flow of blessing, fear is likely at the root. Yet, that's why Paul reminds us that The Lord provides seed to sow and bread for food. God gives us what we need and enough for us to sow a seed. Make sure that when you're blessed, you also keep the blessings flowing to others. Don't eat your seed! A great example of this cycle is when we give to the poor.

"He who has pity on the poor lends to the LORD, And He will pay back what he has given."
- Proverbs 19:17

When we give to the poor, we should give liberally and without reserve. Freely we have received, so freely we should give away. When we allow fear of lack or stinginess to hinder our giving, we prevent the Lord from being able to use us as vessels of generosity and blessing. This scripture says that when we give to the poor, it is like we are letting God borrow from us. Do you think the Lord would be unfaithful to pay back what He owes? Absolutely not! As the verse above says, "He will pay back what he has given." In other words, stop worrying! You'll be repaid in full for the generosity you've shown. Therefore, don't hold back! Be generous.

Georgian Banov of Global Celebration has been a spiritual father and friend to me for many years. I went with him on a mission trip to Bulgaria and was excited to serve him and the vision of the trip. I was also very excited to learn and glean from their ministry and how they bless the gypsy people. One part of that trip that impacted me was the huge feast they prepared for the village. I had never seen anything like it before.

They invested an enormous amount of time and money to purchase one ton of watermelons, bread, and sheep. Using about twenty-four massive pots to cook fatted sheep stew, they were able to feed about eight thousand people. It was an incredible night of celebration, worship, and generosity. I looked over at Jonathan from my team and told him, "We have to start doing this. This is amazing!" It was awesome to see so many people being fed, but being a leader of a ministry myself, I understood the cost that went into accomplishing something like that. That feast wasn't cheap, and the extravagant generosity was truly inspiring!

"He who gives to the poor will not lack, But he who hides his eyes will have many curses."
- Proverbs 28:27

The Bible is clear: we will never go without if we are giving to the poor. If we're cold, stingy, and selfish, not only do we exclude ourselves from this promise, but this verse says we actually invite curses upon ourselves. When I read verses like this and see extravagant giving like what I saw Georgian, Winnie, and their team do in Bulgaria, it makes me excited to do the same!

Unity

"Now all who believed were together, and had all things in common, and sold their possessions and goods, and divided them among all, as anyone had need. So continuing daily with one accord in the temple, and breaking bread from house to house, they ate their food with gladness and simplicity of heart."
- Acts 2:44-46

I don't know about you, but when I look at the majority of the modern Western Church, I don't see the same picture as I do in these verses. The Early Church was so united that they would sell their belongings to help provide for one another. No one had any need because they were taken care of! This concept is foreign to many believers today because we are more influenced by the culture around us, which promotes self-reliance and self-sufficiency. Why would we worry about ourselves when we can trust in the Lord instead, believing that when we freely give, we will receive?

The Early Church understood that giving brings a far greater blessing than receiving. When we live in the selfless love of Jesus, we don't need to worry about ourselves. Giving becomes natural because we know He meets our needs. When we trust Him, we will see opportunities to give and excitedly say, "Oh, you need something? Here you go!" Paul even instructs the Corinthian believers to be prepared to give.

"On the first day of the week let each one of you lay something aside, storing up as he may prosper, that there be no collections when I come."

- 1 Corinthians 16:2

In simple terms, Paul is telling them to have a savings account for their giving. He doesn't talk about personal savings accounts, 401K's, or retirement funds. He doesn't warn them about getting old one day so they can save money to take care of themselves when they can't work anymore. Instead, he teaches them to save money so that when there are needs that come, they are already prepared to give. Do you see the difference? One is focused on preserving self, while the other is focused on honoring others. It's not just simply about meeting needs; it's about showing honor.

The reality is that, according to Jesus, while we're here on Earth, poverty will always be around. Jesus Himself says that the poor will always be among us (see John 12:8). We have to be careful of being more moved by need than we are by the leading of the Lord. If I spent my whole life chasing needs to meet, I wouldn't have much of a life, nor would I be able to focus on specific assignments God has placed before me. The key is to be led by the Lord and to give out of honor, not necessarily out of need.

> *"For as many as are led by the Spirit of God,*
> *these are sons of God."*
> *- Romans 8:14*

There is a difference between giving and being led to give. Sometimes, we like to give, but when God tries to lead us to give, we don't want to. You may wonder if you will still reap a harvest if you sow seeds the gardener doesn't tell you to sow. If they're sown in faith, of course! However, I've seen that the seeds I'm specifically led to sow always bear a greater harvest. When we understand heaven's principles of generosity and blessing and follow the Lord's leading, we'll sow seeds that bear much fruit.

Whenever I've been led to sow a seed, it has always brought about a great harvest. Several years ago, when I began to go deeper into this message of generosity and sowing and reaping, the Lord led me to sow a $1,000 seed into the 12 most impactful people and ministries in my life. At the same time, He told me to write a list of 12 things that I was believing for and expecting. So, I sowed and, over time, I saw almost everything come to pass!

However, I know I wouldn't have seen this happen if I hadn't followed His lead.

God is the best farmer and knows the best soil for us to sow our seed into. When we allow Him to lead us, we let Him tell us where we should plant our seeds to receive the best harvest. Because of this, every time I sow a seed He leads me to sow, I expect a great harvest!

To be clear, I'm not saying you should only give when God tells you to. There is a place for giving out of your desire to sow and to be a blessing. After all, that is what we've been made to do. However, when we sow out of obedience and yield to His leadership, the harvest is always much greater. He is the Lord of the harvest.

I remember one day, I received a fundraising phone call from a ministry I wasn't very familiar with. Before the phone call went long enough for me to hear their plan or vision, I heard the Lord tell me to give $100. About 7 minutes later, the representative finished their fundraising presentation and asked me if I'd be willing to give $34. I asked if I could give $100 instead and proceeded to give the amount the Lord had spoken to me. Later that week, I received a check from a random person for $1,000! When I saw that, I heard the Lord say, "When you listen to me and obey, do not underestimate what I will do."

Keep the Current Flowing

In everything, just continue to give. Be a farmer and develop a lifestyle of constant sowing. It may be as simple as buying someone a meal, donating to someone's mission trip, or getting someone an intentional gift. The principle is the same either way. We are destined to be generous givers. Keep the river flowing. Don't allow it to dam up because of your fear, control, or stinginess. As long as you continue giving generously, having faith, and being led by the Lord, the current of blessing will continue to flow. Show honor through generosity, and be prepared to reap the harvest that comes! We're called to be blessed so that we can be a blessing to those around us. We're called to prosper.

Part 4

Called to Prosper

Chapter 8

Next Level

I'll never forget when I worked at a mental health facility in my 20s. My friend and I would get off around ten or eleven every night and get Wendy's. You may think it's no big deal, but we would fight for the bill. At that time, that was what I was able to afford, and though it may have just been cheap fast food, it was still an opportunity for me to be generous.

That's why I love what Paul teaches in 2 Corinthians 9:11 so much. He says that we are enriched *so that* we can be generous, not just now and then, but "on every occasion" (NIV). Every opportunity to be generous is one to be seized. Today, you may be able to pay for someone's meal at Wendy's, but tomorrow, you may be able to pay someone's rent. I was excited to pay for my friend's meals because I wanted to be a blessing. I also knew that when I gave, I would be blessed as well.

There are levels to giving. There was a time when sowing $50 was a large amount. As you grow, the Lord blesses your finances, and you start giving $100, then $250, then $500, then $1,000, then $5,000, then $10,000, etc. You start getting excited about what's possible. You start wondering what the limit is. Is there even a limit? The journey of upgrading to the next level is meant to be exciting, full of greater opportunities to sow and even greater opportunities to reap a harvest.

Abundant Harvest

It may be helpful if you have some context about my life before the Lord taught me about living in abundance and prosperity. I didn't always want to write a book on generosity. I actually used to be very put off by preachers who talked about this. In fact, years ago, when I was a youth leader, there were times I would warn the guys I was discipling about offering messages. One time, in particular, I had driven some of them to a revival meeting. I wanted them to be encouraged and inspired by the ministers who were there. However, because I was familiar with these preachers, I also knew they were really big into prosperity and preached messages about generosity that challenged people to give more.

As soon as we pulled up to the parking lot, I opened my middle console before we even got out of the car and said, "Everyone, leave your wallets here. Trust me, you'll thank me later." Sure enough, when the preacher got to the offering message, they made a big ask, challenging the congregation to sow a large seed. When the service ended, the guys thanked me because I helped them save their money. It's ironic because now, years later, God's Word has corrected my mindset about this.

One year, my team and I were invited to minister at a church on the East Coast. They hosted a conference themed going to the "Next Level." There were several guest speakers, and each one taught different topics regarding this theme, such as going to the next level in your spiritual walk with God, leadership skills, relationships, identity in Christ, etc. During one of the sessions, I was asked to give the offering message.

I had given countless offering messages before, but I had never done what I was about to do that day. Before getting up to the stage, I heard the Lord tell me to share this with the congregation: "If you want to go to the next level in your finances, you have to go to the next level in your giving. You need to give more than you've ever given before."

Anyone who knew me knew that I was not that guy. I was not the preacher to talk a ton about this subject or tell people to give more money from the pulpit. However, God was working in me, and even though I used to judge those kinds of preachers before, what I didn't understand at the time was how much God truly wants us to live in abundance by walking in generosity. Now, my life has changed. I've started reaping a harvest from the seeds I've sown. Years ago, I would have been very resistant toward the way I'm living now—giving and living in prosperity.

When I shared what the Lord said at that conference, I thought, "I can't say this and not do it myself, or else I'd be a hypocrite." I knew I needed to get to the next level in my own finances. So, that night, I sowed the largest seed I had ever given in one gift up to that point. It was a stretch, but I believed the Lord would bless it and bring a great harvest.

Two months later, I was speaking with my accountant, and he told me, "Daniel, have you seen how much additional income you have made in the last couple of months?" Because I don't always like to pay a ton of attention to the numbers, I wasn't aware. Sure enough, though, after looking over my finances with him, we realized that in those two months following that conference, I received $18,000 *more* than my regular income!

I don't share this to boast about myself but to boast about the goodness of God and the reality that He is a good Father eager to bless His children. We have to understand this if we want to experience the abundance He has in store for us. His Word is true, and He is not a man that He should lie (see Num. 23:19). You get what you believe, and when you believe His Word, it works!

If you want to experience a large harvest, you have to give a large seed. 2 Corinthians 9:6-7 in The Passion Translation says, "A stingy sower will reap a meager harvest, but the one who sows from a generous spirit will reap an abundant harvest." Greater generosity opens the door to greater prosperity. So, when you choose to believe the Lord and have faith in Him, watch what will happen!

As you experience greater blessings, your faith will grow. As your faith grows, you can expect even greater things. The more you expect the Lord to do greater things, the more likely you are to take risks. The more you take risks, the more you give God something to work with. By sowing cautiously and putting all your eggs in one basket, you limit God's ability to move.

When you read the parable of the sower in Mark 4, you see the sower doesn't sow seeds in just one type of soil. He sows into many different types of soil. He flings his seed anywhere and everywhere it will land. The sower is a representation of how God gives. We should learn from Him and set ourselves up to sow anywhere, anytime, and any amount we can.

That being said, I'm not instructing you to give your money away if you're in debt. I've seen people act foolishly and give rather than choose to be diligent and pay off their debt. That's no different than when people attempt to buy their blessing. One of the biggest problems people have with the prosperity message is that it seems like some people try to twist God's arm with their giving.

Just like control and submission can look similar, buying a blessing and sowing a seed can look very similar. I sow because I love, and in the process of sowing and loving, I expect. If I were trying to buy a blessing, I would be trying to manipulate God rather than deal with the heart issue behind my lack. Simon the sorcerer tried to buy the anointing, and that didn't work out so well for him (see Acts 8:9-25).

Remember, just as much as we shouldn't give only to receive, we also shouldn't give without expecting to receive. Giving, when you have a generous heart, becomes common sense. So does abundance.

Think about it: if you have a farm and are planting a bunch of seeds, you're going to reap an abundant harvest. You don't need to worry if there will be enough for you. That's called having a poverty mentality. Know that the seeds you sow are coming back pressed down, shaken together, and running over because you sowed in faith, trusting Him.

Eat the Bread

2 Corinthians 9:10 says that in addition to seed for sowing, the Lord also provides the bread for food. There is a time to focus on giving, and there is also a time to rest, eat, and enjoy the blessings of the Lord. He gives us more than enough and loves us so much that He desires that we enjoy it.

"People spend their youth trying to gain money and when they are old they spend the money trying to gain youth."
-John Maxwell

Some people wait till the end of their lives before they start enjoying themselves. As much as the Lord calls us to be diligent sowers, it also needs to be clear that He desires that we enjoy the blessings of life He's given us. We give Him glory when we enjoy His goodness. I don't know about you, but I want to enjoy my life and make every day count. Carpe diem; seize the day!

It's not that I think we should be frivolous or irresponsible. To me, everything is about value. I choose to be wise with how I spend money on myself, my wife, and the ministry. I do this because I want to be a faithful steward of the finances God has entrusted to me. I don't mind spending or investing money, but I hate wasting money. That being said, I don't live in worry and am not afraid to spend money if the value or need is there.

I know there are times the Lord calls us to sow. When it is that time, I'm eager to participate because I get to partner with Him. Not only that, but I get to be blessed as a result. However, when the Lord says it's time to eat and He provides the bread to enjoy, you can bet that I will take Him up and enjoy it!

No Limits

"Now to Him who is able to do exceedingly abundantly above all that we ask or think, according to the power that works in us."
- Ephesians 3:20

Sometimes, it's tempting to set low expectations of the Lord. To the natural mind, it makes sense to dream small dreams and place limits on God, but with God, all things are possible (see Matt. 19:26)! He has no limits and can exceed anything and everything we could ever ask or think. The Amplified Bible says it like this: "infinitely beyond our greatest prayers, hopes, or dreams." Wow! What would happen if we renewed our minds to think with no limitations?

Start dreaming about what your life would be like with no limits on money or resources. How would you live? What would you do? If your mind immediately goes to what you would do for yourself, you have to renew your mind. The first thing that should come to your mind is how you would give to the Lord and how you would bless others. It's called having a prosperous mindset.

When your mind is focused on surviving, self-preservation, or meeting your own needs, you will live in lack. Your mindset attracts what you will experience. Cycles of lack and greed aren't broken by hoarding up for yourself. They are broken by giving more away! Remember, you are not the lord of your life. When you seek His kingdom first, He will take care of you.

"Do not lay up for yourselves treasures on earth, where moth and rust destroy and where thieves break in and steal; but lay up for yourselves treasures in heaven, where neither moth nor rust destroys and where thieves do not break in and steal. For where your treasure is, there your heart will be also."

- Matthew 6:19-21

I once heard a minister share his conviction that he would not spend on himself what he hasn't sown into God's kingdom first. So, for example, if he saw a suit that he really liked, but it cost more than he'd ever invested into the kingdom of God, he wouldn't buy it. It was a convicting and powerful statement.

If you think about it, it should concern us if we're spending a bunch of money on clothes or other things but not giving the

Lord at least the same amount. If anything, it reveals where our priorities are. Where you put your money is where your heart is. Are your money and heart more toward serving yourself or serving the Lord and blessing others?

For me, it's easy to sow into ministry and Gospel transformation because that's where my heart is. My heart is for the Lord's will to be done on earth as it is in heaven, so when I see ministries producing fruit for His kingdom, I'm eager to sow seeds. If that means I don't spend as much on myself, then so be it. He blesses me abundantly above and beyond my needs anyway.

"And my God shall supply all your need according to His riches in glory by Christ Jesus."
- Philippians 4:19

When you understand that He takes care of your needs according to His riches, what is there to worry about? It's time to let the Lord bring you beyond just your needs. He wants to take you to the next level. Whether in your finances, health, relationships, or mind and emotions, God wants to prosper you in every area of your life. Jesus came so that we would have life more abundantly (see John 10:10), but the key to following Him and His plans is walking by faith and trusting Him.

Chapter 9

Living by Faith, Not by Sight

Over the years, I've grown and learned so much about the Lord's desire for us to live honorable, generous, and ultimately prosperous lives. One thing that helped me tremendously was when I met with a friend who had a thriving ministry and businesses that were growing. He shared stories about His financial increase and how God was using Him to be a blessing. From my perspective, it seemed like he had no worries about finances; he had everything he wanted. I looked at him and asked, "How do you get to the place where finances aren't a concern anymore?" He quickly responded, "Your problem is you want to live where you don't need to have faith."

You see, I admired the blessings that came in but failed to recognize the increase in responsibility and additional expenses that came with the blessing. When increase comes in the areas of business, ministry, and relationships, there is always a greater level of faith and responsibility required. My friend needed to trust the Lord for more every month; he had way more people to lead than I did and way more problems to solve. To live at a greater level of provision requires a greater level of faith in God.

"For we walk by faith, not by sight."
- 2 Corinthians 5:7

I often say that faith is spelled T-R-U-S-T. Paul points out in 2 Corinthians 5:7 that we live by faith and not by sight. That means we don't live by looking at the circumstances in front of us. We look to Jesus and trust the promises He's given to us in His Word. We're called to prosper, but living in kingdom prosperity is impossible without faith in God.

God works in such a way that you will always need to rely on Him. As soon as you receive what you need for the level you're at, He'll call you to do something greater. You'll never be static when you're fully going after everything you're called to in Him. You'll continually be growing. The Bible refers to the believer as an oak of righteousness, a tree planted by the streams of living water, and branches of the vine, which is Jesus. Plants are always growing. The bigger the plant, the more water it needs. In the same way, whatever work God has given us will always require more resources to grow.

When I first started Grace Place, it began with one discipleship house of nine guys. Now, years later, it's grown to become a church and a ministry that travels around the world, providing resources to the Body of Christ with media, books, and online courses. The amount of trust needed to steward the first house was much less than it is now. In the beginning, it was just me leading. I was able to cook, preach, administrate, and take care of almost everything on my own. Now, because of how much the ministry has grown, we have staff and a leadership team who faithfully carry the vision forward to go far beyond what I could do alone. Today, the amount of money I'm believing for far exceeds the original budget of the first Grace Place discipleship house. We are trusting God now more than ever, but I know He will continue to be faithful. He has always provided before, and I know He will do it again.

The Testimony

"...the testimony of Jesus is the spirit of prophecy."
- Revelation 19:10

As we follow the Lord, there may be temptations to be discouraged when things don't turn out the way we thought they should have. However, we don't have to be discouraged; we can be encouraged by what He has done already. God is no respecter of persons. If He does it for one person, He'll do it for another. The way we grow in faith is by continually looking at what Jesus has done. The testimony of what Jesus has done prophesies what He can and will do again.

I'll never forget when, years ago, the Lord blessed me with a new car. At the time, I was driving a beat-up Camry with duct-taped mirrors. A friend called me one day and asked, "Hey, what's wrong with your car?" It was out of the blue and caught me off guard, but I explained to them how my car had a lot of issues. She responded, "That's interesting because the Lord woke me up last night and told me to give you $10,000 for a car!" Because of this blessing, I was able to replace my Camry with a new SUV. Not only that, but the blessing continued to multiply. Every few years, I was able to sell my car to get a new one, and each time, I've been blessed to receive more than what I paid for it, which enabled me to get the newer model!

Years later, I saw that friend again. I told her, "Hey, you're the reason this whole thing began in the first place!" It's amazing how the Lord works full circle. Not only did He miraculously provide me with a new car, but He also allowed her to see how the seed she sowed had grown into many new cars! When I look at my car now, I'm reminded of God's blessing. It's a testimony that I meditate on and thank the Lord for.

Just like I have thought about that testimony many times since, I encourage you to take your testimonies and think about them, write them down, testify to others, and so on. A creative way I've stewarded what the Lord has done in my life is by making videos. I have my video team film every event and trip we do so we can create recap videos of each trip and testimony that takes place. I love to share these videos on social media, in churches, and with friends. Not only am I encouraged when I watch them, but the testimony of what He's done in and through me encourages others, too.

Testimonies don't have to be exclusive to what the Lord has done in your life. If you're believing the Lord for land to build a church, but you've never had Him give you land before, then you'll want to find testimonies of how He's given other people land. If you're believing the Lord for a new car, find testimonies of people who have been given cars.

Seeing what He's done in other people's lives will build your faith in what He can do in yours. There is no way to walk in true prosperity without faith because what He's called you to do will always be impossible without Him. As you meditate on testimonies of what God has done, let them encourage you to press forward into all He wants to do. When you raise your faith and expectation, you'll start believing for His blessing to expand beyond your life into the lives of future generations.

Leaving a Legacy of Prosperity

"A good man leaves an inheritance to his children's children..."
- Proverbs 13:22

Prosperity is meant to extend beyond just the here and now. As amazing as it is to walk in the blessing of God, how much more amazing would it be to leave an inheritance of prosperity for your offspring? The question is, what do you want your legacy to be? When your children, grandchildren, and great-grand-children remember you one day, what would you want them to remember? What would you want them to know for themselves?

As you've learned more about the importance of honor and generosity, my hope for you would be that you would pass those principles on to everyone you influence. This may be your biological children, or it may be people you disciple. Regardless of who it is, you have the opportunity to pass this wisdom along to others.

There are no limits to what He can do in and through your life. As you walk in biblical prosperity, watch as He expands your influence beyond your own life to impact the world around you!

Chapter 10

Corporate Prosperity

"Then Moses summoned Bezalel and Oholiab and every skilled person to whom the Lord had given ability and who was willing to come and do the work. They received from Moses all the offerings the Israelites had brought to carry out the work of constructing the sanctuary. And the people continued to bring freewill offerings morning after morning. So all the skilled workers who were doing all the work on the sanctuary left what they were doing and said to Moses, "The people are bringing more than enough for doing the work the Lord commanded to be done." Then Moses gave an order and they sent this word throughout the camp: "No man or woman is to make anything else as an offering for the sanctuary." And so the people were restrained from bringing more, because what they already had was more than enough to do all the work."

- Exodus 36:2-7 NIV

In the book of Exodus, Moses received detailed instructions from the Lord on the building of His tabernacle. Whether it was the color of the threads used for the curtains, the exact measurement of each precious metal or gemstone, or the specific spices He wanted to be used for the oil, it was an elaborate and precise assignment. When Moses shared the vision and instructions with the people, they immediately responded by contributing their offerings. In fact, as this passage describes, they continued to bring in so much that Moses had to restrain them from giving any more. They had more than enough!

There is a place we're called to live in that is abundantly more than we even need. We've discussed how the Lord wants to bless us personally. In addition to this, we've learned how He wants to bless others through us. The next level the Lord is calling the Church into is corporate prosperity—a place of such collective abundance that we may even need to be restrained from giving as the Israelites were. Even now, some churches take more money in one offering than others do in multiple years because the people understand the grace that comes in giving.

Can you imagine? Instead of constantly searching for the next handout, the Body of Christ can walk in overflowing generosity and extravagant provision. Imagine the resources coming in the moment the Lord gives an assignment. Instead of being stingy and reluctant to give, the Church can give cheerfully and lavishly.

Over the years, I've loved inviting guest speakers to minister at our Grace Place Family Nights. Our ministry and team have been blessed to enjoy some incredible times in the presence of God because of them. However, blessing them in return was equally important to me as inviting them. Even in some of our earlier years, we may have only had 20-30 people present, but no matter how small we were, it was always important to me that we were generous to those who came.

Growing up, I remember hearing my pastor share how the Lord spoke to him, saying, "If you honor those I send you, I'll send you those I honor." Over the years, that phrase has always stuck with me. I've taken it seriously and have made it a strong emphasis in our culture to honor our guests by being generous with our offerings. What's funny is that on several occasions, I've heard from some of our guest ministers that the offerings they received from us were larger than what they'd received from larger churches or ministries. Despite how few of us there may have been, we didn't allow that to stop us from being generous. I believe this is how God wants us all to live.

We're called to be so generous that people are surprised! Instead of expecting cheap and stingy offerings, people should expect large offerings when Christians give. To take it even further, the blessing and prosperity of the Church should extend past the four walls and impact the world around us!

Society of Prosperity

"When the righteous prosper, the city rejoices; when the wicked perish, there are shouts of joy."
- Proverbs 11:10

As we discussed earlier, God desires that the whole earth would be blessed through His people. He wanted to bless the earth through His relationship with Adam and Eve. That's why He told them to be fruitful and multiply. They were meant to spread His blessing to the whole world. The same was true for the Israelites. God wanted to bless the nations of the world through them. His plan has never changed! He still wants to bless the world through His Church. So, when we prosper, as His Body, the blessing should cause the cities we live in to be blessed as well.

God is not ashamed to bless His people. He's a God of extravagance in all He does. Our families, businesses, and churches should start to reflect this. When we grab ahold of this message of prosperity, we will see an increase, and it will be massive! Instead of thinking that the blessing is only for ourselves, we have to know that it's by this favor and increase that God wants to bless the city around us. It's time we start allowing His grace to promote us.

Many people are surprised when they have a place of favor or an open door. Usually, this is because they weren't expecting it. However, we should expect it! In the same way that we expect someone to get healed when we pray, we should expect to have a place of influence.

God promised His people that He would set them high above all the nations of the earth. He said that all the blessings will come upon them and overtake them because they obeyed the voice of the Lord (see Deut. 28:1-2). God was telling them to expect the blessing—to anticipate that it wouldn't just come on them but overtake them.

When we anticipate favor and promotion in everything we do, we'll start thinking and strategizing outside the world's definition of normal. We'll expect our businesses not only to prosper but also to be on the cutting edge. We'll anticipate our children to grow strong in the Lord and full of His power. We'll expect our ministries, churches, and relationships to explode with the abundance and provision of the Lord. What if instead of being intimidated by challenges, we started thinking: *Where God guides, He provides. Where He's taking me, miracles and testimonies await. God's calling me to something great because I was never meant to live a normal life!*

He Adds No Sorrow

"The blessing of the LORD makes one rich,
And He adds no sorrow with it."
- Proverbs 10:22

In all of this talk of prosperity, you may be asking, "Why would I want to be wealthy when I've seen a lot of rich people who are still depressed, angry, and miserable?" It's a valid question, and my simplest response is that those people are probably not walking in the blessing of the Lord.

Some people may have gotten rich, but their wealth came with a lot of sorrow. Why is that? Often, it's because their wealth was gained through unrighteous means. Proverbs 10:2 says, "Treasures of wickedness profit nothing, But righteousness delivers from death." The devil will always attempt to counterfeit everything the Lord creates. Where the blessing of God brings wealth with joy and satisfaction, the treasures of wickedness bring sorrow and ultimately profit nothing. Not only that, but the Bible says that the wealth of the wicked is saved for the righteous (see Prov. 13:22).

There is absolutely nothing to gain from serving self or following the wisdom of the world. On the other hand, when we walk in the ways of God, I can guarantee that we will be blessed because He always prospers His people who are submitted to His leadership. The more blessed we are, the more we can be a blessing to the world around us, causing it to be in our cities as it is in heaven!

Advancing the Kingdom

What would it look like if God were the mayor of your town? How would the streets look? How would the poor be treated? What new businesses and services would He allow in? What sort of change would take place? The only way to know is to see how He rules and governs heaven. The Bible says there is no weeping, pain, or sorrow. The streets are made of gold. There's abundance everywhere you look. If you know what your city lacks, then why not do everything you can to change it?

"...how God anointed Jesus of Nazareth with the Holy Spirit and with power, who went about doing good and healing all who were oppressed by the devil, for God was with Him."
- Acts 10:38

Some of my close friends pastor a church in a smaller city in California. When they first started, they took this scripture to heart. They didn't initially know how to heal those oppressed by the devil, but they knew how to do good. They wanted to look and act like Christ in their community. Because of this, they took action. They found out dozens of children were being taken from their mothers because they were born in prison. They stepped in, and families from their church took care of the children while their mothers served out their sentences. Then, upon release, they returned the children to their mothers.

They then heard that the most marginalized people group in their community was single mothers. They would be taken advantage of at every turn. When they went to get their cars fixed, they'd be charged through the roof for basic repairs. In response to this need, they had mechanics in their church that volunteered to work on single mom's cars for free.

It also came to their attention that there were openings for chaplains in their community. Three of their pastors became the Police Department, Fire Department, and Sheriff chaplains. So, when a crisis came about, they could step in. They desired to be the hands and feet of Jesus. As He had poured His love upon them, they wanted to pour that out into their community. Every step along the way, they had abundant provision to fulfill God's call on their life.

When Covid shutdowns were happening, they received a call from their local government saying they had been deemed non-essential and had to be shut down. The government was okay with letting bars, casinos, and vape shops stay open, but not churches. My pastor friend laughed and said, "We're not closing our doors. We are more essential than you are. Our church feeds the poor, helps people recover from drug addictions, and serves the city in countless other ways." They weren't "non-essential." They were very essential! Every time a need presented itself, multiple people in their church stepped up to meet the need. Out of all the things they were led to do for their city, God always came through and provided the resources to accomplish it.

Take Action

God will always resource what He gives us vision for. In the same way that my friends were led by God to make a change, I believe the Lord has placed a vision in your heart as well. You may have seen a need, but it's greater than what you currently have. Thankfully, you've also seen the generous heart of God, and you know He has more than enough to make His vision happen. The only missing step is taking action.

If you need a financial breakthrough, ask the Holy Spirit where you should be sowing seed! God isn't just going to make the vision happen for you. He wants you to believe His words and begin taking steps of faith. If we want to see Him move, we have to take action by giving in faith!

The Bible is filled with people who partnered with the Lord in faith to see His vision come to pass. They took His words and put them into action. It wasn't until Moses lifted his staff that the Red Sea split. It wasn't until the Israelites blew the trumpet that the walls of Jericho fell. It also wasn't until Jesus came in the flesh to die and rise again that our sins were forgiven.

The main difference between those who see God move mightily in their life and those who don't is their action to take what He's said and execute it in faith. Jesus taught His disciples that the sick would recover if they laid their hands on them (see Mark 16:18). They would have never seen the sick healed if they hadn't followed what He said. The same is true for prosperity.

How do we expect to prosper if we're not willing to listen to His Word and honor by giving generously? We must all ask ourselves: Am I willing to hear His Word and take action?

I don't think you're reading this book because you're unwilling to take action. I believe you take the Word of God seriously. The good news is that it's impossible to follow what He says and not see a mighty harvest of blessing in your life. As you're blessed, allow that blessing to go far past your own life to the world around you. When you take action, you will see His kingdom come and His will be done on earth as it is in Heaven!

Conclusion

Many in the Church today have developed a mindset that ignores money altogether. The God they portray loves and cares for you but seems to turn a blind eye when the bills are due at the end of the month. If God doesn't care about money, why is the Word full of it and why did Jesus, the express image of God, talk about money so much? Did you know that in Scripture there are around 500 verses on prayer and less than 500 verses on faith, but there are over 2,000 scriptures that talk about money and possessions? In fact, around a third of Jesus' parables reference the same topic. The only subject He taught about more was the Kingdom of God.

Why would someone who cared nothing about money teach so much about it? Why would the Lord declare in Haggai 2:8, "The silver and gold is mine"? Why would He say, "For every beast of the forest is Mine, And the cattle on a thousand hills. I know all the birds of the mountains, And the wild beasts of the field are Mine" (Psalm 50:10-11)? Could it be that the God of the Bible is different than we've been led to believe?

The Lord declares Himself to be El Shaddai, the God of more than enough. More than enough of *what?* Does God only provide us with an abundance of good feelings? Does He only promise to bless us spiritually? Or does the God of more than enough promise an abundance of material provision and tangible blessings to those who love Him and follow His commands?

"Beloved, I pray that you may prosper in all things and be in health, just as your soul prospers."

- 3 John 1:2

When John wrote this, he wasn't talking about a concept of spiritual or emotional prosperity. He was praying that their physical bodies would be healthy and that they would tangibly prosper in all things. It is the same with our heavenly Father.

God paid for us to be healthy by the stripes on His back (see Is. 53:5). He also became poor so that we could become rich (see 2 Cor. 8:9). God doesn't want us to be dumb; He wants us to be wise. He doesn't want us sick; He paid for our healing. He doesn't want us to be poor, so He made a way for us to prosper and abound in His blessing.

We in the Body of Christ aren't called to live from one handout to the next. Our lives are meant to consist of more than just getting by. The Lord made us to be lenders, not borrowers (see Deut. 15:6). God's plan for us is to prosper. He desires that the kingdoms of this world would become the kingdom of our God (see Rev. 11:15). He desires that His people would be generous, as He is generous. He calls us to be faithful farmers who sow in faith and reap in abundance. When we trust God's Word, putting it into practice by sowing in faith, we will reap a mighty harvest.

It's time for the Body of Christ to take the Lord at His Word by stepping out of the system of debt and decline. It's time for us to step into the prosperity He has called us to. We must walk in faith, trusting that what He says is true—it is more blessed to give than receive! God so loved the world that He *gave*. When we are generous, we look just like Him. Biblical honor, generosity, and prosperity have been shrouded in mystery, but not any longer. It's time for the *Lost Art of Generosity* to be found!

An Opportunity to Sow

It would be a disservice to you if I didn't encourage you to sow. Don't wait for another time. Seize this moment to give! Think of people God has placed in your life who you can honor. Ask the Holy Spirit what you should give, and follow that.

As you give with a heart that is unto the Lord, I'm more than confident that He will multiply your seed into a mighty harvest for you, your family, your business, and your ministry. If you would like to sow into Grace Place Ministries, follow the ways to give listed below.

Ways To Give

Online:

GracePlacePartner.com

Cash or Check:

Grace Place Ministries

8201 E 41st St.

Sioux Falls, SD, 57110

Zelle:

Name: Grace Place Ministries

Email: finance@graceplaceredding.com

Text to Give:

Text "give" to 833-783-1971

Scan Here

Appendix

Scriptures on Honor, Generosity, and Prosperity

Honor

Matthew 6:24

"No one can serve two masters; for either he will hate the one and love the other, or else he will be loyal to the one and despise the other. You cannot serve God and mammon."

1 Timothy 6:10 KJV

"For the love of money is the root of all evil..."

Matthew 15:4

"For God commanded, saying, 'Honor your father and your mother'; and, 'He who curses father or mother, let him be put to death.'"

Malachi 1:6-8 NIV

"'A son honors his father, and a slave his master. If I am a father, where is the honor due me? If I am a master, where is the respect due me?' says the Lord Almighty. 'It is you priests who show contempt for my name. But you ask, 'How have we shown contempt for your

name?' 'By offering defiled food on my altar.' But you ask, 'How have we defiled you?' 'By saying that the Lord's table is contemptible. When you offer blind animals for sacrifice, is that not wrong? When you sacrifice lame or diseased animals, is that not wrong? Try offering them to your governor! Would he be pleased with you? Would he accept you?' says the Lord Almighty."

Malachi 3:10-11 NASB 1995

"'Bring the whole tithe into the storehouse, so that there may be food in My house, and test Me now in this,' says the LORD of hosts, 'if I will not open for you the windows of heaven and pour out for you a blessing until it overflows. Then I will rebuke the devourer for you, so that it will not destroy the fruits of the ground; nor will your vine in the field cast its grapes,' says the LORD of hosts."

Psalm 37:4 NIV

"Delight yourself also in the LORD, And He shall give you the desires of your heart."

Proverbs 3:9-10

"Honor the LORD with your possessions, and with the firstfruits of all your increase; so your barns will be filled with plenty, and your vats will overflow with new wine."

Matthew 10:41 BBE

"He who gives honour to a prophet, in the name of a prophet, will be given a prophet's reward; and he who gives honour to an upright man, in the name of an upright man, will be given an upright man's reward."

Matthew 6:31-33

"Therefore do not worry, saying, 'What shall we eat?' or 'What shall we drink?' or 'What shall we wear?' For after all these things the Gentiles seek. For your heavenly Father knows that you need all these

things. But seek first the kingdom of God and His righteousness, and all these things shall be added to you."

2 Samuel 24:24

"Then the king said to Araunah, 'No, but I will surely buy it from you for a price; nor will I offer burnt offerings to the Lord my God with that which costs me nothing.' So David bought the threshing floor and the oxen for fifty shekels of silver."

Mark 12:41-44

"Now Jesus sat opposite the treasury and saw how the people put money into the treasury. And many who were rich put in much. Then one poor widow came and threw in two mites, which make a quadrans. So He called His disciples to Himself and said to them, 'Assuredly, I say to you that this poor widow has put in more than all those who have given to the treasury; for they all put in out of their abundance, but she out of her poverty put in all that she had, her whole livelihood.'"

Genesis 14:18–20

"Then Melchizedek king of Salem brought out bread and wine; he was the priest of God Most High. And he blessed him and said: 'Blessed be Abram of God Most High, Possessor of heaven and earth; And blessed be God Most High, Who has delivered your enemies into your hand." And he gave him a tithe of all."

1 Chronicles 29:12-14 NIV

"Wealth and honor come from you; you are the ruler of all things. In your hands are strength and power to exalt and give strength to all. Now, our God, we give you thanks, and praise your glorious name. But who am I, and who are my people, that we should be able to give as generously as this? Everything comes from you, and we have given you only what comes from your hand."

Titus 3:8

"This is a faithful saying, and these things I want you to affirm constantly, that those who have believed in God should be careful to maintain good works. These things are good and profitable to men."

Jeremiah 17:7-8

"Blessed is the man who trusts in the Lord, and whose hope is the Lord. For he shall be like a tree planted by the waters, which spreads out its roots by the river, and will not fear when heat comes; but its leaf will be green, and will not be anxious in the year of drought, nor will cease from yielding fruit."

Deuteronomy 8:18

"And you shall remember the Lord your God, for it is He who gives you power to get wealth, that He may establish His covenant which He swore to your fathers, as it is this day."

GENEROSITY

Acts 4:33-37

"And with great power the apostles gave witness to the resurrection of the Lord Jesus. And great grace was upon them all. Nor was there anyone among them who lacked; for all who were possessors of lands or houses sold them, and brought the proceeds of the things that were sold, and laid them at the apostles' feet; and they distributed to each as anyone had need. And Joses, who was also named Barnabas by the apostles (which is translated Son of Encouragement), a Levite of the country of Cyprus, having land, sold it, and brought the money and laid it at the apostles' feet."

Matthew 6:1-4

"Take heed that you do not do your charitable deeds before men, to

be seen by them. Otherwise you have no reward from your Father in heaven. Therefore, when you do a charitable deed, do not sound a trumpet before you as the hypocrites do in the synagogues and in the streets, that they may have glory from men. Assuredly, I say to you, they have their reward. But when you do a charitable deed, do not let your left hand know what your right hand is doing, that your charitable deed may be in secret; and your Father who sees in secret will Himself reward you openly."

Leviticus 27:30

"And all the tithe of the land, whether of the seed of the land or of the fruit of the tree, is the LORD's. It is holy to the LORD."

1 Corinthians 16:2

"On the first day of the week let each one of you lay something aside, storing up as he may prosper, that there be no collections when I come."

Psalm 37:26 NLT

"The godly always give generous loans to others, and their children are a blessing."

Matthew 10:42

"'And whoever gives one of these little ones only a cup of cold water in the name of a disciple, assuredly, I say to you, he shall by no means lose his reward.'"

James 1:27

"Pure and undefiled religion before God and the Father is this: to visit orphans and widows in their trouble, and to keep oneself unspotted from the world."

Isaiah 58:10-11

"If you extend your soul to the hungry and satisfy the afflicted soul,

then your light shall dawn in the darkness, and your darkness shall be as the noonday. The Lord will guide you continually, and satisfy your soul in drought, and strengthen your bones; you shall be like a watered garden, and like a spring of water, whose waters do not fail."

1 John 3:17 NIV

"If anyone has material possessions and sees a brother or sister in need but has no pity on them, how can the love of God be in that person?"

Romans 12:13 NIV

"Share with the Lord's people who are in need. Practice hospitality."

Luke 12:33 NIV

"Sell your possessions and give to the poor. Provide purses for yourselves that will not wear out, a treasure in heaven that will never fail, where no thief comes near and no moth destroys."

James 2:15–16

"If a brother or sister is naked and destitute of daily food, and one of you says to them, 'Depart in peace, be warmed and filled,' but you do not give them the things which are needed for the body, what does it profit?"

Deuteronomy 15:7–8

"If there is among you a poor man of your brethren, within any of the gates in your land which the LORD your God is giving you, you shall not harden your heart nor shut your hand from your poor brother, but you shall open your hand wide to him and willingly lend him sufficient for his need, whatever he needs."

Proverbs 22:9 NLT

"Blessed are those who are generous, because they feed the poor."

Proverbs 18:16

"A man's gift makes room for him, And brings him before great men."

Deuteronomy 15:10 NLT

"Give generously to the poor, not grudgingly, for the LORD your God will bless you in everything you do."

2 Corinthians 8:1–5 NIV

"And now, brothers and sisters, we want you to know about the grace that God has given the Macedonian churches. In the midst of a very severe trial, their overflowing joy and their extreme poverty welled up in rich generosity. For I testify that they gave as much as they were able, and even beyond their ability. Entirely on their own, they urgently pleaded with us for the privilege of sharing in this service to the Lord's people. And they exceeded our expectations: They gave themselves first of all to the Lord, and then by the will of God also to us."

Philippians 4:15–17

"Now you Philippians know also that in the beginning of the gospel, when I departed from Macedonia, no church shared with me concerning giving and receiving but you only. For even in Thessalonica you sent aid once and again for my necessities. Not that I seek the gift, but I seek the fruit that abounds to your account."

1 Chronicles 29:6-9

"Then the leaders of the fathers' houses, leaders of the tribes of Israel, the captains of thousands and of hundreds, with the officers over the king's work, offered willingly. They gave for the work of the house of God five thousand talents and ten thousand darics of gold, ten thousand talents of silver, eighteen thousand talents of bronze, and one hundred thousand talents of iron. And whoever had precious stones gave them to the treasury of the house of the LORD, into the

hand of Jehiel the Gershonite. Then the people rejoiced, for they had offered willingly, because with a loyal heart they had offered willingly to the LORD; and King David also rejoiced greatly."

1 Kings 10:13 NIV

"King Solomon gave the queen of Sheba all she desired and asked for, besides what he had given her out of his royal bounty. Then she left and returned with her retinue to her own country."

John 3:16

"For God so loved the world that He gave His only begotten Son, that whoever believes in Him should not perish but have everlasting life."

Romans 8:32

"He who did not spare His own Son, but delivered Him up for us all, how shall He not with Him also freely give us all things?"

James 1:17

"Every good gift and every perfect gift is from above, and comes down from the Father of lights, with whom there is no variation or shadow of turning."

Matt. 10:8

"Freely you have received, freely give."

2 Corinthians 9:7

"So let each one give as he purposes in his heart, not grudgingly or of necessity; for God loves a cheerful giver."

Proverbs 11:25 NLT

"The generous will prosper; those who refresh others will themselves be refreshed."

2 Corinthians 9:10-11 NIV

"Now he who supplies seed to the sower and bread for food will also supply and increase your store of seed and will enlarge the harvest of your righteousness. You will be enriched in every way so that you can be generous on every occasion, and through us your generosity will result in thanksgiving to God."

Proverbs 19:17

"He who has pity on the poor lends to the LORD, And He will pay back what he has given."

Proverbs 28:27

"He who gives to the poor will not lack, But he who hides his eyes will have many curses."

Acts 2:44-46

"Now all who believed were together, and had all things in common, and sold their possessions and goods, and divided them among all, as anyone had need. So continuing daily with one accord in the temple, and breaking bread from house to house, they ate their food with gladness and simplicity of heart."

2 Corinthians 9:6-7 TPT

"A stingy sower will reap a meager harvest, but the one who sows from a generous spirit will reap an abundant harvest."

Ephesians 3:20

"Now to Him who is able to do exceedingly abundantly above all that we ask or think, according to the power that works in us."

Hebrews 13:16

"But do not forget to do good and to share, for with such sacrifices God is well pleased."

Proverbs 11:24 NIV

"One person gives freely, yet gains even more; another withholds unduly, but comes to poverty."

2 Corinthians 8:12 NIV

"For if there is first a willing mind, it is accepted according to what one has, and not according to what he does not have."

2 Corinthians 8:7 NLT

"Since you excel in so many ways—in your faith, your gifted speakers, your knowledge, your enthusiasm, and your love from us—I want you to excel also in this gracious act of giving."

Luke 6:30

"Give to everyone who asks of you. And from him who takes away your goods do not ask them back."

Psalm 37:21

"The wicked borrows and does not repay, But the righteous shows mercy and gives."

Luke 3:11

"He answered and said to them, 'He who has two tunics, let him give to him who has none; and he who has food, let him do likewise.'"

Proverbs 21:25–26

"The desire of the lazy man kills him, For his hands refuse to labor. He covets greedily all day long, But the righteous gives and does not spare."

Proverbs 3:27

"Do not withhold good from those to whom it is due, When it is in the power of your hand to do so."

Prosperity

Jeremiah 29:11 NIV

"'For I know the plans I have for you,' declares the Lord, 'plans to prosper you and not to harm you, plans to give you hope and a future.'"

Genesis 13:2

"Abram was very rich in livestock, in silver, and in gold."

Nehemiah 8:10

"Then he said to them, 'Go your way, eat the fat, drink the sweet, and send portions to those for whom nothing is prepared; for this day is holy to our Lord. Do not sorrow, for the joy of the LORD is your strength.'"

Deuteronomy 2:7

"For the LORD your God has blessed you in all the work of your hand. He knows your trudging through this great wilderness. These forty years the LORD your God has been with you; you have lacked nothing."

Deuteronomy 30:15-16

"See, I have set before you today life and good, death and evil, in that I command you today to love the Lord your God, to walk in His ways, and to keep His commandments, His statutes, and His judgments, that you may live and multiply; and the Lord your God will bless you in the land which you go to possess."

Joshua 1:5, 7-8

"No man shall be able to stand before you all the days of your life; as I was with Moses, so I will be with you. I will not leave you nor forsake you. Only be strong and very courageous, that you may observe to do according to all the law which Moses My servant commanded you; do

not turn from it to the right hand or to the left, that you may prosper wherever you go. This Book of the Law shall not depart from your mouth, but you shall meditate in it day and night, that you may observe to do according to all that is written in it. For then you will make your way prosperous, and then you will have good success."

1 Kings 2:3
"And keep the charge of the Lord your God: to walk in His ways, to keep His statutes, His commandments, His judgments, and His testimonies, as it is written in the Law of Moses, that you may prosper in all that you do and wherever you turn."

1 Chronicles 22:13
"Then you will prosper, if you take care to fulfill the statutes and judgments with which the Lord charged Moses concerning Israel. Be strong and of good courage; do not fear nor be dismayed."

2 Chronicles 20:20
"So they rose early in the morning and went out into the Wilderness of Tekoa; and as they went out, Jehoshaphat stood and said, "Hear me, O Judah and you inhabitants of Jerusalem: Believe in the Lord your God, and you shall be established; believe His prophets, and you shall prosper."

Psalm 122:6-7
"Pray for the peace of Jerusalem: "May they prosper who love you. Peace be within your walls, prosperity within your palaces."

2 Chronicles 26:5
"He sought God in the days of Zechariah, who had understanding in the visions of God; and as long as he sought the Lord, God made him prosper."

2 Chronicles 31:21

"And in every work that he began in the service of the house of God, in the law and in the commandment, to seek his God, he did it with all his heart. So he prospered."

Job 36:11

"If they obey and serve Him, they shall spend their days in prosperity, and their years in pleasures."

Psalm 1:1-3

"Blessed is the man who walks not in the counsel of the ungodly, nor stands in the path of sinners, nor sits in the seat of the scornful; but his delight is in the law of the Lord, and in His law he meditates day and night. He shall be like a tree planted by the rivers of water, that brings forth its fruit in its season, whose leaf also shall not wither; and whatever he does shall prosper."

Psalm 34:10

"The young lions lack and suffer hunger; but those who seek the Lord shall not lack any good thing."

Psalm 35:27

"Let them shout for joy and be glad, who favor my righteous cause; and let them say continually, "Let the Lord be magnified, who has pleasure in the prosperity of His servant."

Psalm 68:19

"Blessed be the Lord, who daily loads us with benefits."

Psalm 112:1-9

"Praise the Lord! Blessed is the man who fears the Lord, who delights greatly in His commandments. His descendants will be mighty on earth; the generation of the upright will be blessed. Wealth and riches

will be in his house, and his righteousness endures forever. Unto the upright there arises light in the darkness; he is gracious, and full of compassion, and righteous. A good man deals graciously and lends; he will guide his affairs with discretion. Surely he will never be shaken; the righteous will be in everlasting remembrance. He will not be afraid of evil tidings; his heart is steadfast, trusting in the Lord. His heart is established; he will not be afraid, until he sees his desire upon his enemies. He has dispersed abroad, he has given to the poor; his righteousness endures forever; his horn will be exalted with honor."

Psalm 115:11-16

"You who fear the Lord, trust in the Lord; He is their help and their shield. The Lord has been mindful of us; He will bless us; He will bless the house of Israel; He will bless the house of Aaron. He will bless those who fear the Lord, both small and great. May the Lord give you increase more and more, you and your children. May you be blessed by the Lord, who made heaven and earth. The heaven, even the heavens, are the Lord's; but the earth He has given to the children of men."

Psalm 132:12-18

"If your sons will keep My covenant and My testimony which I shall teach them, their sons also shall sit upon your throne forevermore. For the Lord has chosen Zion; He has desired it for His dwelling place: "This is My resting place forever; Here I will dwell, for I have desired it. I will abundantly bless her provision; I will satisfy her poor with bread. I will also clothe her priests with salvation, and her saints shall shout aloud for joy. There I will make the horn of David grow; I will prepare a lamp for My Anointed. His enemies I will clothe with shame, but upon Himself His crown shall flourish."

Proverbs 8:17-21

"I love those who love me, and those who seek me diligently will find me. Riches and honor are with me, enduring riches and righteousness. My fruit is better than gold, yes, than fine gold, and my revenue than choice silver. I traverse the way of righteousness, in the midst of the paths of justice, that I may cause those who love me to inherit wealth, that I may fill their treasuries."

Proverbs 10:2-6

"Treasures of wickedness profit nothing, but righteousness delivers from death. The Lord will not allow the righteous soul to famish, but He casts away the desire of the wicked. He who has a slack hand becomes poor, but the hand of the diligent makes rich. He who gathers in summer is a wise son; he who sleeps in harvest is a son who causes shame. Blessings are on the head of the righteous, but violence covers the mouth of the wicked."

Proverbs 13:4

"The soul of a lazy man desires, and has nothing; but the soul of the diligent shall be made rich."

Proverbs 28:13

"He who covers his sins will not prosper, but whoever confesses and forsakes them will have mercy."

Proverbs 28:25

"He who is of a proud heart stirs up strife, but he who trusts in the Lord will be prospered."

Ecclesiastes 5:19

"As for every man to whom God has given riches and wealth, and given him power to eat of it, to receive his heritage and rejoice in his labor—this is the gift of God."

Isaiah 1:19

"If you are willing and obedient, you shall eat the good of the land."

Philippians 4:19

"And my God shall supply all your need according to His riches in glory by Christ Jesus."

Acts 14:17

"Nevertheless He did not leave Himself without witness, in that He did good, gave us rain from heaven and fruitful seasons, filling our hearts with food and gladness."

Exodus 36:2-7 NIV

"Then Moses summoned Bezalel and Oholiab and every skilled person to whom the Lord had given ability and who was willing to come and do the work. They received from Moses all the offerings the Israelites had brought to carry out the work of constructing the sanctuary. And the people continued to bring freewill offerings morning after morning. So all the skilled workers who were doing all the work on the sanctuary left what they were doing and said to Moses, "The people are bringing more than enough for doing the work the Lord commanded to be done." Then Moses gave an order and they sent this word throughout the camp: "No man or woman is to make anything else as an offering for the sanctuary." And so the people were restrained from bringing more, because what they already had was more than enough to do all the work."

Proverbs 11:10

"When the righteous prosper, the city rejoices; when the wicked perish, there are shouts of joy."

Deuteronomy 28:1-14

"Now it shall come to pass, if you diligently obey the voice of the Lord your God, to observe carefully all His commandments which I command you today, that the Lord your God will set you high above all nations of the earth. And all these blessings shall come upon you and overtake you, because you obey the voice of the Lord your God: Blessed shall you be in the city, and blessed shall you be in the country. Blessed shall be the fruit of your body, the produce of your ground and the increase of your herds, the increase of your cattle and the offspring of your flocks. Blessed shall be your basket and your kneading bowl. Blessed shall you be when you come in, and blessed shall you be when you go out. The Lord will cause your enemies who rise against you to be defeated before your face; they shall come out against you one way and flee before you seven ways. The Lord will command the blessing on you in your storehouses and in all to which you set your hand, and He will bless you in the land which the Lord your God is giving you. The Lord will establish you as a holy people to Himself, just as He has sworn to you, if you keep the commandments of the Lord your God and walk in His ways. Then all peoples of the earth shall see that you are called by the name of the Lord, and they shall be afraid of you. And the Lord will grant you plenty of goods, in the fruit of your body, in the increase of your livestock, and in the produce of your ground, in the land of which the Lord swore to your fathers to give you. The Lord will open to you His good treasure, the heavens, to give the rain to your land in its season, and to bless all the work of your hand. You shall lend to many nations, but you shall not borrow. And the Lord will make you the head and not the tail; you shall be above only, and not be beneath, if you heed the commandments of the Lord your God, which I command you today, and are careful to observe them. So you shall not turn aside from any of the words which I command you this day, to the right or the left, to go after other gods to serve them."

Matthew 7:11

"If you then, being evil, know how to give good gifts to your children, how much more will your Father who is in heaven give good things to those who ask Him!"

Genesis 12:2-3

"I will make you a great nation; I will bless you and make your name great; And you shall be a blessing. I will bless those who bless you, and I will curse him who curses you; And in you all the families of the earth shall be blessed."

Matthew 6:19-21

"Do not lay up for yourselves treasures on earth, where moth and rust destroy and where thieves break in and steal; but lay up for yourselves treasures in heaven, where neither moth nor rust destroys and where thieves do not break in and steal. For where your treasure is, there your heart will be also."

Proverbs 10:22

"The blessing of the LORD makes one rich, And He adds no sorrow with it."

Proverbs 13:22

"A good man leaves an inheritance to his children's children, But the wealth of the sinner is stored up for the righteous."

3 John 1:2

"Beloved, I pray that you may prosper in all things and be in health, just as your soul prospers."

2 Corinthians 8:9

"For you know the grace of our Lord Jesus Christ, that though He was rich, yet for your sakes He became poor, that you through His poverty might become rich."

About Grace Place

Grace Place Ministries is a discipleship community fueled by a passion to see God's people walk out their identity in Christ and establish His Kingdom upon the earth. We are committed to developing mature Christian leaders through one-on-one mentoring, building family through weekly gatherings, and providing leadership opportunities designed to facilitate connection and growth. We travel frequently to minister around the world and create resources to build up the Church in her righteous identity.

Vision

Mature sons and daughters
established in their identity in Christ,
spreading the Gospel of grace and truth.

Mission

Disciple young adults.
Minister around the world.
Resource the nations.

Discipleship is our Mission; Will you Join Us?

Now, more than ever, the body of Christ needs to arise and shine. The world is searching for answers and is in need of an encounter with God's love and truth. Who will raise up a generation to bring answers our world is desperately seeking?

"For the earnest expectation of the creation eagerly waits for the revealing of the sons of God."
– Romans 8:19

Whether it is a young man or woman needing a mentor or an entire church seeking the resources to disciple their community, you can make an impact!

Become a Partner with Grace Place Ministries:

Go to:
www.graceplacepartner.com

Grace Place Ministries

ADDITIONAL RESOURCES

THE LOST ART OF DISCIPLESHIP
God's Model for Transforming the World

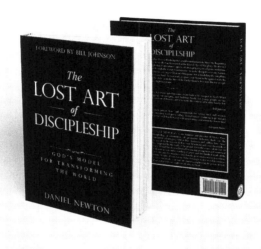

Discipleship is not a man-made idea. It is God's design for world transformation. *The Lost Art of Discipleship* is the uncovering of heaven's blueprints for remodeling the kingdoms of the earth into the Kingdom of our God. In his cornerstone book, Daniel Newton pulls from 20 years of experience in discipleship. As you read, prepare your heart to be ignited with the fires of revival that once swept the globe as in the days of the Early Church. It is time for the people of God to arise and shine for our light has come!

Available at www.GracePlaceMedia.com
@GracePlaceDiscipleship

ADDITIONAL RESOURCES

THE LOST ART OF DISCIPLESHIP
Workbook

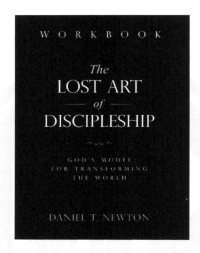

Enrich your understanding and increase your mastery of God's model for world transformation. This companion workbook to *The Lost Art of Discipleship* book is filled with exclusive content, in-depth exercises, and practical coaching to introduce a lifestyle of discipleship in your day-to-day walk. Whether you have been following the Lord for years or recently surrendered your life to Jesus, this manual breaks down the Great Commission and equips you for a life of fruitfulness!

Available at www.GracePlaceMedia.com
@GracePlaceDiscipleship

THE LOST ART OF DISCIPLESHIP
Online Course

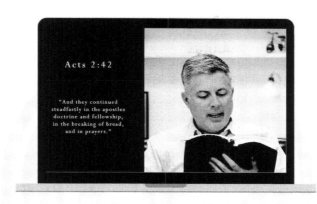

You can live the Great Commission. Every believer is called to embrace Jesus' final command: to make disciples... and this interactive online course is designed to take you even deeper into the rich content taught in *The Lost Art of Discipleship*.

Whether you are wanting to position yourself as a son or daughter, lead as a father or mother, or create a culture of discipleship, this course is for you! Rediscover the lost art with over five hours of video content, practical teaching, quizzes, and supernatural activations from Daniel Newton.

Available at www.GracePlaceMedia.com
@GracePlaceDiscipleship

Additional Resources

Immeasurable
Reviewing the Goodness of God

You are made in the image of the Miracle Worker,
designed to manifest His glorious nature.
Immeasurable: Reviewing the Goodness of God is a collection
of 100 real-life stories of salvation, healing, deliverance,
signs and wonders, reconciliation, and provision. Every
miracle is a prophetic declaration of what God wants to
do in, through, and for someone just like you.

Available at www.GracePlaceMedia.com
@GracePlaceDiscipleship

ADDITIONAL RESOURCES

TRUTH IN TENSION
55 DAYS TO
Living in Balance

NEVER GIVE UP
The Supernatural Power of
Christ-like Endurance

Other Titles

ALL THINGS
Have Become New, Work Together for Good, Are Possible

IT IS FINISHED
Exposing the Conquered Giants of Fear, Pride, and Condemnation

THE LOST ART OF PERSEVERANCE
Rediscover God's Perspective on Your Trials

THE LOST ART OF FAITH RIGHTEOUSNESS
Rediscover How Believing Leads to Receiving

THE LOST ART OF FASTING
Cultivating a Deeper Hunger for God

THE LOST ART OF SELFLESS LOVE
Freely Receive. Freely Give.

THE LOST ART OF REST
The Only Thing Worth Striving For

THE LOST ART OF EXCELLENCE
The Supernatural Character of Christ

THE LOST ART OF FRIENDSHIP
God's Design for Authentic Connection

THE LOST ART OF CONFRONTATION
From Conflict to Connection

THE LOST ART OF MEDITATION
You Become What You Behold

THE LOST ART OF DELIVERANCE MINISTRY
Make Casting Out Demons Normal Again

THE LOST ART OF PRAYING IN TONGUES
Get Out of Your Head and Into the Spirit

ADDITIONAL RESOURCES

GP MUSIC: BEGINNINGS

Everyone has a story. Most people don't realize that God doesn't just want to improve their story. He wants to rewrite it. Beginnings offers a fresh start, a new focus. This worship album invites you into the core anthems of grace and truth which have impacted us at Grace Place.

Our prayer is that this album helps you lay down your past mistakes, your present circumstances, and your future worries in order to lift both hands high in surrender to the One you were created to worship. We ask that you join us in a new beginning — an exciting start to a life filled with perseverance, focus, and surrender.

Available at www.GracePlaceMedia.com
@GracePlaceDiscipleship

KEEP US UPDATED

We would love to connect with you and hear about everything God has done in your life while reading this book! We also would love to hear how we can be praying for you. Submit a testimony or prayer request by going to www.GracePlaceRedding.com/mytestimony

STAY CONNECTED WITH GRACE PLACE

Are you interested in staying up to date with Grace Place Ministries and receiving encouraging resources via email?

VISIT OUR WEBSITE:
www.GracePlaceSiouxFalls.com

SIGN UP FOR OUR NEWSLETTER AT:
www.GracePlaceRedding.com/newsletter

FOLLOW US ON SOCIAL MEDIA:
@GracePlaceDiscipleship